The SPORTS HEROES Library

SUPERSTARS
STOPPED SHORT

Nathan Aaseng

 Lerner Publications Company • Minneapolis

ACKNOWLEDGMENTS: The photographs are reproduced through the courtesy of: pp. 4, 25, Los Angeles Lakers and Photography, Inc., Inglewood, California; pp. 7, 26, 31, 32, 42, 45, 48, 53, Wide World Photos, Inc.; pp. 8, 12, National Baseball Hall of Fame and Museum, Inc.; pp. 15, 16 (top left), Los Angeles Dodgers; p. 16 (top right), San Francisco Giants; p. 16 (bottom left), Atlanta Braves; p. 16 (bottom right), Cincinnati Reds; p. 18, Phoenix Suns; p. 23, Phoenix Suns, Richard Wisdom; pp. 34, 40, Cleveland Cavaliers; p. 39, Department of Photography & Cinema, The Ohio State University; p. 54, New York Jets; p. 56, University of California at Berkeley; p. 58, Richard Pilling; p. 62, Minnesota Twins; pp. 66, 68, 70, New England Patriots.

Cover photograph: Doug Pizac, California Angels

LIBRARY OF CONGRESS CATALOGING IN PUBLICATION DATA

Aaseng, Nathan.
  Superstars stopped short.

  (The Sports heroes library)
  SUMMARY: Outlines the short careers of a group of exceptional athletes who were blocked from reaching the top through no fault of their own.

  1. Athletes—United States—Biography—Juvenile literature. [1. Athletes] I. Title. II. Series.

GV697.A1A217   796'.092'2 [B] [920]   81-12431
ISBN 0-8225-1326-9   AACR2

Manufactured in the United States of America

International Standard Book Number: 0-8225-1326-9
Library of Congress Catalog Card Number: 81-12431

1 2 3 4 5 6 7 8 9 10 91 90 89 88 87 86 85 84 83 82

Contents

Connie Hawkins had to wait eight years before the NBA allowed him to display moves such as this soaring lay-up.

Introduction

Coaches in athletics often talk excitedly about a "can't-miss" prospect. That is an athlete who is so well built, coordinated, and intelligent and with such great desire and dedication that he or she cannot miss being a star. Those can't-miss people seem to have it made. All they have to do is to use their natural skills, and they will automatically enter into a world of glory, high salaries, and easy living.

Unfortunately, however, there is no such thing as a can't-miss prospect. Sometimes we look upon sports stars so much as heroes that we forget they are also human. But they are, and no matter how talented they are or how hard they work, there is no guarantee that they will succeed. Like all other humans, athletes can get hurt, they can get sick, and they die. And they can also be victims of accidents, injustice, and mistakes.

We hear about the successful athletes all of the time. Those stars get so much attention that we rarely hear about the tremendous athletes whose careers, through no fault of their own, ended suddenly. It has been estimated that for every successful story in athletics, there are hundreds of sadder tales. A Duke University study followed the careers of 900 high school baseball players who were talented enough to attract and sign professional contracts. Of that total, only 20 actually made it to the major leagues. And only five of them lasted as long as five years in the pros. Even the top football players in the country are lucky if they play more than three years in the National Football League.

Athletes know that there are great risks involved in choosing a sports career. And the successful ones know that, no matter how talented they might be, they owe their fame and fortune to a great deal of luck. One twist of fate and the world might never have heard of Muhammad Ali, Roger Staubach, Eric Heiden, or Reggie Jackson.

This book contains stories of athletes who were not so fortunate. While their names might not be familiar, they include some of the greatest athletes in the world. If life were totally fair, these people would have been on the covers of magazines, and millions of fans would have tuned in to watch them perform. But all of them were stopped short—each in a different way.

Unfortunately, the world was never able to see these athletes at the height of their power and talent. And their stories show that the world of sport is not a dream world but simply a small part of life. They are a reminder that athletes are human and that the success and fame of an athletic career can be a *very* risky goal to shoot for.

Was Eddie Hart the world's fastest human in 1972? Shortly before disaster struck, he easily won this trial heat of the Olympic 100-meter dash.

Josh Gibson waits to unleash the power that made him the most feared slugger of the Negro Leagues.

1
Josh
Gibson

In 1887 the St. Louis Browns scheduled an exhibition game against a group of black players. Just before the game, however, most of the St. Louis regulars suddenly became "too injured to play," according to the Browns, and the game was cancelled. For the next 60 years, blacks were not allowed on the same field with major league baseball teams. It was not until 1959, when the Red Sox signed Pumpsie Green, that all of the league teams included blacks on their roster.

The prejudice against blacks hurt baseball in many ways. Fans were cheated out of seeing some of the finest players of their time. And owners of losing teams missed out on signing players who could have almost guaranteed them a winning club.

But most of all, the ban on blacks hurt the players, including slugging catcher Josh Gibson.

Joshua Gibson was born in Buena Vista, Georgia, in 1911. His family moved to Pittsburgh when he was 10, and there Josh took part in the city's many neighborhood sports. Stocky and powerful, young Josh Gibson considered the local Negro League club, the Homestead Grays, his heroes. He longed for a chance to play with them, and he prepared himself by joining the semi-pro Crawford Colored Giants. The Giants received no salaries for playing. Instead they would pass a hat among the onlookers at their games for whatever money they could get.

In 1930 the Homestead Grays' catcher hurt his finger during a game. The Grays immediately sent a cab to fetch Gibson, whom they had heard was a fine young player. When the 18-year-old arrived, he showed them an unusual batting style. His upper body was so strong that he did not have to stride into a pitch. Instead he swung at it flat-footed. Even then he could hit the ball so far that he became an immediate star.

One of the most important games for the Grays that year was against the New York Lincoln Giants in Yankee Stadium. Josh crashed a 500-foot home run that rivaled the longest ever hit by the great

Babe Ruth. That hit was the first of many legendary clouts for Gibson. Once in a game in Monessen, Pennsylvania, he hit a baseball so far that the mayor of the town stopped the game to measure the distance. The tape showed the ball had traveled 512 feet! Another time Gibson hit a line drive so hard that it split the shortstop's hand underneath his fielding glove.

Josh's most spectacular hit of all, however, came when he was fooled by a pitch. He tried to adjust his swing at the last instant, but his left hand slipped off the bat. With only his right hand holding the bat, Josh still drilled the pitch out of the park.

Teams in the Negro Leagues spent nearly every day of the year looking for a game to play. Then when the cold weather arrived, they would pack up and head south to Central America. In countries such as Cuba, Venezuela, and Mexico, they would draw more fans and make more money than they would make in the United States. In the spring they would return north, only to find themselves still second-class ballplayers. For example, the Grays were allowed to use Forbes Field in Pittsburgh for their games. But they were not allowed to dress there. Instead they had to suit up at the YMCA across town.

The power-hitting Gibson won praise from Washington's Walter Johnson who said Gibson was a better catcher than New York Yankee Hall-of-Famer Bill Dickey.

Black players in the United States at that time could not hope to match the salaries of white players. In his prime, Josh Gibson probably reached a salary of about $1,500 a month. While that was a very comfortable living then, it was nowhere near the $80,000 per year figure that Babe Ruth commanded during those years.

In hopes of earning more money, many Negro League stars jumped from team to team. Gibson moved over to the Pittsburgh Crawfords in 1932 and then back to the Grays in 1937. But wherever he went, he would overpower the opposing pitchers. Although there were no official statistics kept for most of the Negro League teams, some of Gibson's achievements have been recorded. In 1930 he blasted 75 home runs, though no one is certain how many games he played in to reach that mark. Three years later, Josh batted .467 for the season with 55 home runs. Many people believe that 1936 was his peak year when he was credited with 84 home runs. Those figures are even more impressive, considering the type of pitching that Gibson faced. Spitballs were perfectly legal then, and Josh often faced pitches that dipped crazily after being sand-papered, cut with razors, or greased with hair tonic.

But despite his incredible power and fine fielding

behind the plate, Josh never received the acclaim he deserved—even within his own league. He was a quiet, serious sort, and he was overshadowed by flashier characters such as fireball pitcher Satchel Paige. But the ballplayers knew what Gibson could do. Even white major leaguers such as Walter Johnson and Dizzy Dean were so impressed with what they saw of him that they called Josh one of the greatest players in baseball. Several major league teams were tempted to take advantage of his great skills, but no one dared to take that important step.

In the later stages of his career, Gibson began to fall into some bad habits. He loved ice cream and beer, and he consumed so much of each that he grew overweight. His health started to fall apart, and in the early 1940s, he was hospitalized several times with mental illnesses. But despite these warning signs, Gibson was unable to change his life. In 1943 he suffered a nervous breakdown.

Josh continued to play baseball, however, and he performed well. But even though he could still hit for a high average, his fearsome power quickly vanished. In 1945 he won the league batting title with an impressive .393 average, but he rarely hit anything but singles.

14

Jackie Robinson broke baseball's 65-year-old barrier against blacks when he signed a minor league contract with the Brooklyn Dodgers in 1945. In 1947 he was named Rookie of the Year, and two years later he was the National League's Most Valuable Player.

That year, 1945, the great breakthrough for black ballplayers finally came. Branch Rickey of the Brooklyn Dodgers signed Jackie Robinson to a minor league contract to pave the way for blacks in the major leagues. But by that time, Josh was too old, and his skills were fading too fast for him to attract any major league offers. In his final season in 1946, he managed to earn a spot on his league's All-Star team.

Roy Campanella

Willie Mays

Hank Aaron

Frank Robinson

16

A year later, Josh Gibson was dead of a stroke at the age of 35. It was a bitter irony that in the year of Josh's death, 1947, Jackie Robinson became the first black called up to the major leagues. Robinson soon shattered all doubt as to the skill of black players, and he won Rookie of the Year honors in the National League.

While many black stars went on to become successful in baseball, Josh Gibson lay unnoticed in an unmarked grave. It was not until 1975 that his baseball skill was recognized, and he was voted into the Baseball Hall of Fame.

By being the first major league team to rely heavily on black players such as catcher Roy Campanella, the Dodgers won seven National League titles between 1947 and 1956. Other talented black players soon joined both leagues. They included Willie Mays who won many games for the Giants during his 22-year career in the 1950s and 1960s with his powerful batting, fielding, and throwing; Hank Aaron who played 23 years in the major leagues and belted 755 home runs to top Babe Ruth's 39-year-old mark of 714; and Frank Robinson who played for 21 years and led both the Cincinnati Reds and the Baltimore Orioles to pennants with his hitting.

Finally free to roam the NBA courts, the "Hawk" fires a short jump shot for the Phoenix Suns.

2
Connie
Hawkins

In the 1960s a gangly, 6-foot, 8-inch youngster dueled the top stars of the National Basketball Association (NBA) in the playgrounds of New York. His incredible moves often made the best players in the world feel like beginners. Kareem Abdul-Jabbar admitted that he had never seen anyone better than this Connie Hawkins, and most players agreed with him.

While others basked in basketball headlines, Hawkins spent most of his time practicing by himself in schoolyards. Connie would have given anything for a chance to play in the NBA. But for eight of his best playing years, Hawkins was banned from the league—a victim of injustice.

Connie was born in Brooklyn, New York, in 1942. He had grown up in a poor, crime-filled neighborhood and had so little money that he owned only one pair of slacks. His father had left him when he was 10. Hawkins' life was not made easier by his scrawny build, which embarrassed him. And on top of that, Connie was so poorly educated that he could barely read, even in high school.

But one thing Connie could do well was to play basketball. He was named a high school All-American, and he was singled out as the top high school player in New York. Also to Connie's credit was the fact that he stayed out of trouble with the law. In fact, he knew so little about the world of crime that he was unaware of the gambling scandals that kept popping up in basketball. Criminals liked to bet heavily against a good team and then pay some of the players to lose the game on purpose. At the age of 18, Connie met Jack Molinas and Joe Hacken, two men who were involved in this kind of activity. But as far as Hawkins knew, they were just a couple of generous men who befriended him.

Connie enrolled at the University of Iowa in 1960 on a basketball scholarship. He had been there only for a few months, however, when he was called back to New York. Investigators claimed that he had helped his two friends get ballplayers to lose games for money. During six straight days of questioning, Hawkins insisted that he was innocent. But he finally became convinced that the police would send him to jail if he did not change his story. So he confessed.

Everyone involved in the gambling scandal protested that Hawkins had known nothing about it. And though Connie was never tried or convicted of anything, he was one of 47 college players banned from both college and NBA play.

After his hearing, Hawkins tried to keep his career going by playing for the Pittsburgh Rens of the American Basketball League. But it did him little good to win the league's Most Valuable Player Award because the league went out of business in his second year. Next Connie tried to tour with the Harlem Globetrotters, but that was not the kind of basketball he wanted to play for a career. By 1966 Hawkins had no job and no place to play. Several NBA teams wanted to sign him, but they were denied permission by the league officials.

In 1967 the American Basketball Association (ABA) was formed as a serious challenge to the NBA. Connie joined the Pittsburgh Pipers and became the league's first star. Despite being forced to play center because of the lack of skilled players

—where his thin body was pounded during every game—Hawkins averaged 26.8 points per game and won the ABA's Most Valuable Player Award. For many fans in the country, that had been their first look at the flashy, swooping style of the "Hawk." Connie had such huge hands that he would flip the ball around with one hand as if it were a softball. His quickness and leaping ability helped him to work free from the best defenders. But the Pipers could not make money in Pittsburgh, and they moved to Minnesota the next season. There Hawkins continued to jam in points from all angles, and he averaged 30 points a game in 1968-69.

During his first season in Minnesota, Hawkins met a writer named Dave Wolf. Wolf listened to Connie's frustrating story of being banned from the NBA. He was shocked at the unfairness and dug into Hawkins' case. Within four months, Wolf had uncovered enough evidence to prove that Hawkins was innocent, and that he had never even known his friends were gamblers. Connie and his lawyers then started a lawsuit against the NBA to force them to let him play in their league. Then just when it seemed he was getting somewhere in his fight to get into the NBA, Hawkins tore some

A Portland player pauses before testing Hawkins' reactions and long arms.

cartilage in his knee. Connie nervously waited to see if the injury would heal and, fortunately, it did.

Finally in 1969, the good news came through. The NBA settled the case out of court and offered Hawkins a fine contract with the Phoenix Suns.

23

Connie slid off his chair and sank to the floor on his knees when he heard the news. Eight years of frustration were finally over. And though he had already lost many of the best years of his career, as well as years of valuable coaching, he was not bitter. Instead he was determined to make use of the time he had left to prove he belonged with the best.

Hawkins quickly proved that he was one of the top offensive forwards in the game. He scored 24.6 points per game and was voted first team All-Pro that year. Though the Suns were a new team in only their second season of play, Connie took them into the play-offs. There he helped his team battle the powerful Los Angeles Lakers down to the wire before losing the series, four games to three.

The Suns won even more the next two years with Connie shooting a solid 21 points per game both years. Then his age and the years of hardship began to take their toll, and his performance began to slide. His scoring dipped to a 16.1 average in 1972-73, and he was traded to the Lakers the following season. There he continued his decline until he finished his career with the Atlanta Hawks in 1976, averaging about 8 points per game.

NBA fans had seen only a brief glimpse of the

Winding down his short career with the Lakers, Connie
backs in toward the basket against the Chicago Bulls.

colorful talent of the Hawk. There simply was not
enough time for Connie to win a championship or
to make much of an impression in the pro record
books. Because of that, he may soon be forgotten
by basketball fans. And perhaps only a few people
will remember that some of the best basketball
ever was played in a New York City schoolyard
when Connie Hawkins was shut out from the pros.

Chi Cheng was at the top of her form in 1970, the year she was named Woman Athlete of the Year by the Associated Press.

3
Chi
Cheng

Young Chi Cheng had never run in a track meet before. But to her classmates in Hsin-chu, Taiwan, she seemed to be an exceptionally fast runner. So she had been chosen to represent her school in a provincial meet. Chi, however, did little to distinguish either herself or her school in that race, and she finished dead last. But instead of being discouraged by her defeat, she took to a track career wholeheartedly. She and her family took running so seriously that her mother made it a point to take her to the temple before her meets.

By the age of 16, Cheng had improved enough to represent Taiwan in the 1960 Olympics in Rome. There she again found herself overmatched by the older, better trained, and more experienced runners, and she finished last in her heat of the hurdles.

Despite such an unspectacular early career, however, Chi was one of the first athletes whom a United States coach noticed on his visit to Taiwan in 1962. The coach, Vince Rees, who had come to help Taiwan's track team to prepare for the Asian games that year, could not help but notice the long-legged Cheng. At 5 feet, 7-½ inches, she stood taller than many of the male athletes. Rees also discovered that Chi had tremendous reactions—twice as fast as a normal person—and the strength to do 60 push-ups. After watching her run, he became convinced that, with top-level training and competition, Cheng could become an outstanding runner. The Taiwan government agreed that Chi could go to the United States to get such training. So in 1963 she moved to California and enrolled in the California public school system.

The intense workouts, however, did not seem to bring any better results for Cheng. Again in 1964 Chi made the Taiwan Olympic team as a hurdler, but once again she was swept aside by the competition. She hurt her leg in the middle of her race and found herself on the sidelines during the finals.

That second Olympic setback did not dampen Chi's confidence, however. She loved to train and race, and she responded to defeats with added determination. Cheng talked to herself before races, challenging and criticizing herself, until by racetime she had practically worked herself into a rage. Sprinters often liked to try and "psych out" their opponents; that is, they would say or do things to distract them and to keep them from doing their best. But when sprinters would try to upset Chi by downgrading her ability, they only succeeded in making her even more angry. Chi thought these tactics were very unsportsmanlike, and she usually saw that they backfired.

During the next years, Cheng continued to improve at sprinting and hurdling until she was a world-class racer in several events. But the hard work took its toll on her body. In 1967 Chi was forced to have an operation to correct a problem with her knee. That next summer, as she was preparing for her third Olympics, she pulled muscles in both legs. Determined to race despite her problems, she won her first Olympic medal by finishing third in the hurdles at the Mexico City Olympics in 1968. She also came close in the 100-meter dash and finished seventh.

As a sore-legged veteran of three Olympics, Cheng could easily have been content with her medal and given up running. But she pressed on, and ran so furiously in her races that she quickly became almost unbeatable in the sprints and hurdles. Looking for new challenges, Chi then began to long jump. And although she hated the distance, she even ran in some 400-meter races.

Beginning in 1969, Chi went on an incredible winning streak. Among her greatest wins that year was the United States Amateur Athletic Union title in the hurdles with a time of 13.7.

By June of the following year, Chi was still picking up speed. Running for the Los Angeles Track Club in a meet in Portland, Oregon, she broke two world records. She opened a huge gap on her competitors in the 100-yard dash, a race usually so close that it required a photo finish. Clad in red shorts for good luck, she blazed the distance in 10.0, a full 3/10th of a second faster than the world record shared by Wyomia Tyus of the U.S.A. and Marlene Matthews of Australia!

Cheng then entered the 220-yard dash, and the outcome of the race was decided before she had even moved out of the turn and into the straightaway. Her time of 22.7 beat Australian Margaret Burvill's world mark by 2/10th of a second. Later that same day, Chi went on to win the 100-meter hurdles.

After earlier breaking two world records in this 1970 meet in Portland, Oregon, Chi settles for an "ordinary" 13.24 win in the 100-meter hurdles.

Although it was her least favorite event, Chi won this 440-yard dash as easily as she had won the sprints.

Chi took every race so seriously that there was no chance of an opponent catching her on an off day. Because of this, from 1969 to 1970 Chi was able to put together a startling record of 119 victories in 121 races over a variety of distances. Altogether she broke or equalled seven world records. At age 26, Chi had become by far the fastest woman in history, and she was honored by the Associated Press as the 1970 Woman Athlete of the Year. She seemed to be capable of some scorching sprint records that would stand for many years.

But Chi's smooth stride was deceiving, for her legs were working anything but smoothly. By the end of the 1970 track season, her legs throbbed terribly. Finally the pain became so great that she could not even walk, and she had to do something drastic. So Cheng entered a hospital for a visit— a visit that would mark the end of her track success.

Chi was hospitalized for two months. Then she went back into training—only this time she did not worry about world records. Instead Chi trained simply to relearn how to walk. To correct her leg problems, the doctors had removed 14 inches of muscle in her left thigh and 11 inches in her right.

After regaining the use of her legs, Chi went into coaching at Redlands University in California. Her brief, two-year reign as the world's top track woman was over, soon to fade into the background. The woman who was so far beyond all of her opponents had been stopped short of ever winning track's top prize—the Olympic gold medal.

There was a time when Witte vs. Jabbar sounded like an interesting match-up—but it never was.

4
Luke
Witte

The giant center had returned to lead the Ohio State University basketball team. He seemed fully recovered from the injuries he had suffered in a brawl earlier in the season. The Ohio State fans hoped that he would soon return to top form and lead their team to repeat their Big Ten championship of the previous season. But though Luke Witte had healed on the outside, something inside of him was not quite the same. The fiery competitiveness, the aggressive play, and the alertness on the court never came back.

Luke was born in 1950, the son of a philosophy professor, Dr. Wayne Witte. Luke grew quickly and had reached almost 7 feet by the end of high school. But despite his height, he was not a beanpole.

Luke was a well-built 240 pounds, and he played with a smoothness and coordination that was rare for someone his size.

Witte was one of the most highly recruited high school players in the state of Ohio in 1969. Among those coaches who tried to attract him was Bill Musselman. Musselman was a successful coach who had relied on defense to turn his Ashland College teams into a small college power. But although Ashland had been successful in recruiting Luke's dad to teach philosophy, they were not able to interest Luke. He turned down Musselman's offer, but that would not be the last time the two would meet.

Witte wanted the challenge of a major college team, so he enrolled at Ohio State. Led by such players as Jerry Lucas and John Havlicek, the Buckeyes had molded some great teams in the 1950s. Luke developed more quickly than expected, and he helped to return the Buckeyes to glory in his sophomore season. The 7-foot wonder kid averaged 19 points and 13 rebounds a game. And he so dominated the area around the basket that Ohio State surprised the experts by winning the Big Ten title with a 13-1 record. Witte sank 56 percent of his shots, a figure that helped Ohio

State to lead the league in shooting percentage. For his efforts, he was named center on the All-Conference team, joining such older stars as future pros Fred Brown and Jim Cleamons.

Before the 1971-72 season, basketball experts were looking for Ohio State to improve on its number 10 national ranking of the previous year. The main reason was Witte, whom *Sports Illustrated* had described as a "well-coordinated battler, certain to improve."

At the start of the Big Ten season, the Buckeyes set out to prove the experts right. They quickly jumped to a 3-0 mark in conference play and prepared for a showdown with their main challenger, the Minnesota Gophers. The Minnesota coach happened to be Bill Musselman, who had quickly built up a large and spirited following at all Gopher home games. The cheers and screams of over 17,000 fans echoed off the walls of the Williams Arena when the Gophers took the floor against Ohio State on January 25, 1972.

The Minnesota coaches, players, and fans knew that in order to beat Ohio State, they would have to stop Witte. But that was much easier said than done. Witte and the Buckeyes controlled the second half and took a 50-44 lead with 36 seconds to go.

Luke was then fouled while driving in for a lay-up, and he fell to the floor. With two foul shots coming, Ohio State's victory seemed certain. The win on their rival's home court would give Ohio State a large advantage in the conference race.

As Luke started to pick himself off the floor, a Minnesota player offered a hand to help. But then he suddenly turned on Witte. The frustrated players and fans on the losing side immediately turned the game into a riot. Ohio State players were attacked, and Witte got the worst of it. He lay on the floor, stunned and battered, until help finally came. Luke was taken to a hospital, so dazed that he could not remember anything that happened after the lay-up attempt. Basketball fans everywhere were outraged, and two of the Minnesota players were suspended from play for the rest of the year.

The Ohio State team struggled without Luke for the next couple of games. When he returned to action, the team hoped that everything would be just as it had been before the brawl. But something was missing, and the Buckeyes lost 4 of their last 10 games and missed out on the conference title. Witte's love of basketball had been severely shaken by the attack, and he was not playing as well as he had before.

A year after their brawl, a sub-par Witte tries a shot over a Minnesota player.

Fans hoped that Witte was finally pulling out of his slump that summer when he did well in the U.S. Olympics basketball trials. Luke was named an alternate to the Olympics team that lost the gold medal to the Soviet Union in a controversial game.

But the Luke Witte who had been All-Big Ten as a sophomore never returned to his former promising

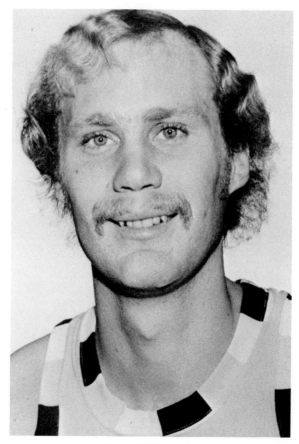
Luke Witte

level of play. During his senior year at Ohio State, he seemed to be just another tall player in the league. His team sunk to an 8-6 mark, and Luke was not mentioned for Big Ten honors that year.

The Cleveland Cavaliers still held out hope that Witte could play as he once did, and they signed him to a contract for the 1973-74 season. He saw action as a reserve and checked into 57 games that year, averaging 4.5 points. Cleveland had hoped that Luke could do better, but that season proved to be the high point of his pro career. He hung on with the Cavaliers until 1977 and finished with a career average of 3.2 points per game.

Basketball had always been an enjoyable game before that 1972 incident in Minnesota. But since that time, the game had lost its fun for Luke, and the fine pro prospect from Ohio State had slowly dropped out of basketball.

Hart's gold medal performance in the 400-meter relay was small consolation for the strange twist of fate that marred his 1972 Olympic stay in Munich.

42

5
Eddie
Hart

The Olympic Games are important to amateur athletes because they are held only once every four years. The highest honor in amateur sports, the Olympic gold medal, is won or lost in a single moment of athletic competition. It is frightening enough for an athlete to think that long years of work could be spoiled if he or she would make one crucial mistake in the Olympics. But even more frustrating is the fact that an athlete might work for four years and then never even get the chance that he or she deserved.

For example, many African nations suddenly pulled out of the 1976 Montreal Games for political reasons. Even more nations, including the United States, did the same in 1980 to protest the policies of the host country, the Soviet Union. But although

43

such decisions must have been heartbreaking to the athletes involved, they could not have been as damaging as a setback involving sprinter Eddie Hart.

Eddie was born in Martinez, California, in 1948. He first became known for his sprinting while at the University of California at Berkeley. In 1970 he swept to victory in the National Collegiate Athletic Association track championships, winning the 100-yard dash in a time of 9.4. The following year the California senior was barely edged out while trying to defend his title, and he had to settle for second place.

After he finished college that year, Eddie seemed to fade from sight on the track scene. Although his top time of 9.3 seconds for 100 yards made him a respected opponent, Hart rarely won any races. But Eddie did not care about winning races in 1971. Instead he was aiming for one big race in the 1972 Olympics. While supporting himself as a graduate assistant at California, he trained hard and refused to rest up for any meets. By the time of the United States Olympic trials in 1972, Eddie had only one major victory to his credit, a first at the Kennedy Games.

At the trials in Eugene, Oregon, Eddie continued

Hart (lane 6) needed a world-record tying run to nip Rey Robinson (lane 1) in the United States Olympic trials in Eugene, Oregon, in 1972.

to have problems winning races. He did not win either of his first two heats, but he ran well enough to qualify for the next round. In the semifinals, he found himself in the middle of a pack of sprinters blazing at world-record speed. Six sprinters all lunged for the finish line at about the same time. Each were awarded a time of 9.9 for the 100 meters—a time that would have tied the world record had it not been disallowed because a strong wind had been behind the runners. Hart was one of five in that group who made the finals.

The chance to run in the Olympics was at stake when the sprinters settled into their blocks for the finals of the 100-meter dash. Rey Robinson, a junior from Florida A&M, was a fast starter, and he tore out of the starting blocks for an early lead. Hart started slowly but surged ahead, gaining on Robinson. The two pounded down the track almost dead even over the final yards. But Hart inched ahead before the finish line, capturing first place and matching the world record with a time of 9.9. Robinson followed so closely that he was awarded the same time.

Hart's performance immediately made him one of the favorites in the 1972 Olympics held that September in Munich, West Germany. Americans were counting on him, and possibly Robinson, too, to carry on the United States' mastery of the sprints. Since 1932 Americans had won all but one 100-meter dash gold medal. They faced a strong challenge, however, from Valery Borzov of the Soviet Union. Borzov had shown such a smooth powerful stride that, before the United States' trials, many thought of him as the best sprinter in the world. But after the speed shown by Hart and Robinson in the trials, experts were no longer so certain.

In their morning heats of the Olympic 100, Hart,

Robinson, and the third United States' sprinter, Robert Taylor, all qualified for the next round. Sprint coach Stan Wright consulted his schedule and told them to be back for their next race at seven o'clock in the evening.

Later that afternoon, the American sprinters were preparing to return to the track when they happened to see a television screen. They saw some men in familiar uniforms settled at the starting line for what was obviously a 100-meter dash. Thinking it was a rerun of the morning races, they paused to watch. Suddenly their world seemed to crash around them as they realized that it was a *live* broadcast of the 100-meter quarterfinals! Their coach had been using a year-and-a-half-old time schedule that had long since been changed. Somehow only the American team had had the wrong time.

Hart and his teammates rushed to the stadium, but he and Robinson had already missed their heats. Taylor barely had time to rush to the starting line, rip off his sweatclothes, and crouch for the start. Without any warm-up, he ran second to qualify for the next round.

United States' officials begged to let their runners race in a later heat, but the request was denied.

With the top two American sprinters on the sidelines, Valery Borzov of the Soviet Union breezed to a win over Robert Taylor in the 100-meter finals.

When it came time for the finals, Eddie Hart was an unenthusiastic spectator amid a crowd of excited fans. He watched Borzov blaze down the track just ahead of Robert Taylor, who finished second. Hart could not help but wonder if he could have beaten Borzov, whose winning time was an unspectacular 10.14 seconds.

Coach Wright took the blame for the mistake, but no one ever explained why the American team was so poorly organized that they had the wrong schedule. Considering the years of effort that had been spoiled, Hart was amazingly calm. He refused to criticize his coach, saying that the blame could not be put on only one man.

Eddie's role in the 400-meter relay held later in the Olympics only served to add to the pain. As the American and Russian runners tore around the track, the American team gradually pulled out to a slim lead. Hart and Borzov waited at the final turn to run the fourth and final leg of the race. Hart grabbed the handoff just ahead of Borzov and took off like a shot around the curve and down the straightaway. Borzov could not gain a step on Hart, and the United States won the gold medal in a record time of 38.19. The run gave further proof that a 100-meter dash between Borzov, Hart, and probably Robinson, too, would have been a thrilling race.

Unfortunately for Hart, no one remembers who wins relay races. But they do remember the 100-yard dash winner because he wins the right to be called the "world's fastest human." And Eddie's hard training to achieve that title was ruined by an incredible blunder over which he had had no control.

In November 1975, Joe Roth (left) was named Back of the Week
by the Associated Press. Playing against the Washington Huskies,
Roth had completed 24 of 36 passes.

6
Joe
Roth

In 1977 Joe Roth was the college quarterback the pro scouts wanted the most. Roth seemed to have everything needed to succeed at the position. He was tall, well built, had a good arm, and was extremely intelligent. He also showed a remarkable ability to keep cool under pressure. But most of the scouts did not know that the pressures of a football game were nothing compared with what the handsome quarterback was quietly going through.

Joe was born and raised in San Diego, California. At Granite Hills High School, his 6-foot, 4-inch, 165-pound build was not well suited for football, and he did not play much until his junior year. Then Joe started to show his skill when his team was facing a tough opponent. Although a driving rain throughout the game made it difficult to handle the ball, Joe was not afraid to throw passes. He tossed the slippery ball for 220 yards and led his team to an easy victory.

The terrible weather, however, must have kept the college scouts away that day. Because when he graduated in 1973, Joe found himself without any major college football offers. So he entered nearby Grossmount Junior College, hoping that after two seasons of junior college play he would be ready for a larger school. During his first season, he did not impress his coaches as more than an average, hard-working player, although his straight-A average showed that he was obviously intelligent.

Roth spent the summer after his freshman year working on a weight-training program to build up his strength. During that time, a mole on his chin started bothering him. When he had it checked out by doctors, they found that Joe had cancer, and they operated on his neck to remove the cancerous tissue. Although the operation was successful and Joe quickly recovered, no one could be certain that he had totally beaten the disease.

Joe took the news of his cancer calmly, and he tried not to let others find out about it. He went back to Grossmount in the fall to play football, and he led his team well. Grossmount went to the

California State Junior College play-offs and capped a great year by taking the championship. Joe was named to several All-American teams and this time the major schools took notice.

By that time, Roth was well aware that there was more to life than football. So he did not want to go to one of the "football factory" colleges that put too much emphasis on the game. Instead he chose the University of California at Berkeley, a school as famous for its academic program as for its athletics. One of the few things that California's football program could boast of was a series of top college quarterbacks. Steve Bartkowski had just left the school to join the Atlanta Falcons as a number one draft choice when Roth came.

Even though Roth had shown great promise at Grossmount, the California coaches refused to simply hand him a starting job. So Joe began the season as a reserve quarterback. But the team showed little offense early in the season and lost their first two games. They were behind again in the third game when they finally turned to Joe for help. Starting from his own five-yard line, Roth led the Golden Bears on a spectacular drive. After moving out to the opposing 41-yard line, he faded back to pass, looking for speedy wide receiver

Many of Roth's bombs went to fleet Wesley Walker, who later went on to star for the New York Jets.

Wesley Walker. Walker had slipped in behind the defense, and Joe fired into his waiting arms for the winning touchdown. The victory ended all talk about keeping Roth on the bench.

In his first start the next week, Joe and his teammates trailed San Jose State late in the game, 24-20. This time it seemed that his last-minute offense was going nowhere. The Golden Bears were thrown backwards and faced a grim third and 22 situation. But Roth fired a first down pass and then teamed up with Walker for another long game-winning pass.

For the first time in years, California's football team was fighting for a Rose Bowl spot. With All-American running back Chuck Muncie (later drafted by the New Orleans Saints) leading the ground attack and Roth and Walker burning defenses on long passes, the Golden Bears were a match for anyone. The Southern California Trojans, one of the top-rated teams in the nation, discovered that one autumn afternoon. With Joe passing for 244 yards, California romped to a surprisingly easy win over Southern Cal on national television.

One week later, Roth took to the field against the highly regarded pass defense of the University of Washington. Joe tore apart the defensive back-field, hitting 24 of 36 passes for another comfortable win. But despite California's 8-3 season, they lost out to UCLA for the Rose Bowl trip.

Based on what they had seen in that one short season, the pros rated Joe as the top college passer going into the 1976 season—ahead of such pros-pects as Tommy Kramer of Rice University, who later played for the Minnesota Vikings. He had grown to a solid 205 pounds and had shown that

Joe Roth

he could throw the long pass without getting inter-
cepted. They were a little disturbed by his showing
that season, however. California fell to a 5-6 mark,
and Joe did not seem to be quite the player that
he had been the year before.

Slowly, the reason for Roth's troubles leaked out.

Joe's cancer had returned. He had tried to keep it a secret so that he would not hurt his chances of being drafted by the pros and so people would not feel sorry for him. But two weeks after the season was over, Joe's cancer was out of control.

Roth still managed to play in the Hula Bowl and the Japan Bowl All-Star games. Friends reported that Joe was as much of an inspiration to them in his last days as when he had been healthy. Surrounded by his teammates, Joe Roth died at home in February 1977. During a time when salary squabbles, strikes, and legal hassles dominated the sports headlines, the story of the courageous Joe Roth was quietly laid to rest.

Bostock slashes another line drive for the Minnesota Twins.

7
Lyman Bostock

Lyman Bostock, Jr., learned a good deal about his father from the newspapers. His father had won press clippings for his play as a first baseman in the Negro leagues. The color barrier had been broken by the time Lyman, Jr., was born in 1950, but by then it was too late for the elder Bostock to play in the major leagues. Young Bostock's parents had separated when he was five, and Lyman had lived as an only child with his mother. Still he was impressed by his dad's success in the world of baseball, and he hoped to be a ballplayer himself some day.

Lyman, however, had no money for equipment. When he and his mother had moved from Birmingham, Alabama, to Los Angeles in 1957, they had a total of $7 on them. Lyman had to get in his practice by throwing rocks in the air and hitting them with a broom handle.

After developing into a fine player in high school, Bostock attended the University of California at Northridge. In 1972 he led his team into the college division World Series. But somehow he was labeled as a player with a "bad attitude," and he was passed over by most pro teams. Bostock went unclaimed through 25 rounds of baseball's free agent draft that year until the Minnesota Twins made him the 596th player selected.

In the minor leagues, Lyman quickly displayed his slashing style of hitting. The only ones who did not care for his attitude were the opposing pitchers who had to dodge his line shots up the middle. Lyman batted .294, .313, and .333, respectively, in his three years of minor league ball. That performance earned him his long-awaited chance to play in the major leagues in 1975.

The thrill of the big leagues wore off in a hurry, however. In an April 1975 game against the Oakland A's, outfielder Bostock sprinted after a deep drive headed for the center field fence. He made a fine catch of the ball and held on as he crashed into the barrier. In the process, he broke his ankle and missed more than a month of playing.

But the folowing year, Bostock began spraying hits all over the field. The Chicago White Sox learned some painful lessons about giving the 6-foot, 1-inch, 170-pounder good pitches to hit. The White Sox had six chances to stop him during one game, and they failed each time. In every appearance at the plate during that game, Lyman found a new way to beat his opponents. His hitting demonstration for the day included a home run, a triple, a double, a single, a sacrifice fly, and a walk for a 17-2 romp.

Other teams studied Bostock closely and noticed that he seemed to hit everything to the middle of the field. But when they shifted their fielders to cover that area, Lyman continued to get his hits. That year his final batting average of .323 captured fourth place in the American League batting race.

It was obvious that the Twins had come up with yet another hard-hitting left-handed batter. First there had been Tony Oliva, who had won three batting titles from 1964 to 1971. Then Rod Carew had taken over, winning the title prior to 1977 in 1969, 1972, 1973, 1974, and 1975. Just as Carew was reaching his hitting peak, Bostock was being groomed to take over.

With Bostock, Carew, and slugger Larry Hisle

A gallery of Twins' hot hitters—Tony Oliva (upper left), Rod Carew (upper right), Lyman Bostock (lower left), and Larry Hisle (lower right). Lyman continued the Twins' fine tradition of hitting started by Oliva in 1964.

62

drilling hits, the Twins kept baserunners busy crossing home plate in 1977. Lyman contributed with a .336 average, second in the league only to Carew. Displaying some hidden power in his thin body, he hit 14 home runs, 12 triples, 36 doubles and scored 104 runs. Lyman was also a valuable team member in that he could play both center field and left field well. Teammates also enjoyed his constant chatter about any subject in the world.

Unfortunately, the Twins' pitching was not strong enough to take advantage of their fine offense. The team faded at the end of the season, and Lyman was starting to get in trouble with Twins' fans and administration over his contract troubles. At the end of the season, Bostock and his close friend, Hisle, decided to test their worth in the free agent market. As two of the finest players to go the free agent route, they found their services were in great demand. Lyman finally signed with the California Angels for over two million dollars, one of the largest contracts of that time.

Whether it was the pressure caused by his large salary or the change of scenery, Bostock suffered through a horrid spring in 1978. He went hitless in his first 14 times at bat to launch him on the first serious slump of his career. Suddenly helpless with his bat, he was still bogged down at a .051 average after 39 trips to the plate. Critics began to nod and say, "See what happens when an athlete gets so much money. He doesn't even try."

But Lyman was more upset than anyone. He tried to give his first month's salary back to the Angels, saying that he had not given them their money's worth. When the Angels refused to accept it, Lyman gave the money to charity.

It was only a matter of time, however, before Bostock broke out of his slump, and line drives started jumping off his bat. By September he had raised his batting average to .296.

That month the Angels flew to Chicago to take on the White Sox. Whenever a road trip took him to Chicago, Lyman liked to visit his uncle in nearby Gary, Indiana. On the evening of September 23rd, while he was riding in a car with his uncle and two friends, another car pulled up beside them. A man pulled out a gun and fired. He was apparently trying to hit one of the others in the car but instead killed Bostock, whom he did not even know.

The baseball world was shocked by Bostock's death. Lyman had been a very likeable man and an athlete destined to be a star hitter. But in a sudden flash, he was gone.

8
Darryl
Stingley

A wide receiver's job in pro football is something like a high-speed chase scene in a movie where the driver is always dodging terrible disaster at the last second. He speeds through the defensive backfield, catching passes and avoiding dangerous tackles. That is especially true on passes thrown to the center of the field. Then the wide receiver must concentrate on catching the ball while defenders rush at him from all angles. Most receivers are so quick that they can make the catches and still stay healthy enough to stay in the game.

But every so often the danger catches up to the quickest of them, as it did to Darryl Stingley. His unusual courage in running dangerous middle-of-the-field pass patterns led to a terrible accident.

Darryl was a city boy born in Chicago, Illinois,

New England's Stingley tries to ignore the close coverage of a
Baltimore Colt defender as he awaits a pass.

in 1951. At John Marshall High School, he was both a fine student and an excellent athlete. Basketball was the big sport at the school, and Darryl was often tempted to throw away his football pads and concentrate only on basketball. But he continued to play football, too, and was so skilled that he was named Chicago's prep player of the year in 1968. His high school credentials included an average of 13 yards per carry and one 4-touchdown game.

Later, at Purdue University, the coaches tried to get the ball to the speedy Stingley as often as they could. There Darryl played wide receiver and flanker and did everything from blocking to running to catching deep passes. He showed a flair for the sudden score in 1971, catching an 80-yard pass against Washington and a 76-yarder against Minnesota. As one of the key men in Purdue's offense, he was often the target of some solid hits by defensive players such as Ohio State's All-American Jack Tatum. But he was able to shake off most tackles and run right back to the huddle.

Although ignored by many All-American rankings, Darryl's playing had impressed the pro scouts. New England liked his speed and all-around skill, and they selected him in the first round of the 1973 draft with a choice they had obtained from

Stingley grabs the kind of high pass that leaves wide receivers open to hard hits.

Stingley's hometown team, the Chicago Bears. Stingley quickly won over the players and coaches with his friendliness, confidence, and quick smile. On his first trip to Boston, Darryl guided fellow number one draft choice Sam Cunningham around the city until Sam could get used to life in the big Eastern city.

The Patriots found Darryl equally useful in 1973, and Darryl never had to worry about not finding playing time. In that rookie season, he caught 23 passes for an average of almost 15 yards a catch. Darryl also took on the risky job of running back punts and kickoffs.

Five weeks into the next season, Darryl was put out of action with a broken arm. But he was back in 1975, putting his speed to use. That year Darryl began to develop into the team's long-pass threat. In 1976 he averaged 18 yards every time he got his hands on a pass, and he improved that mark to 21.8 in 1976. Darryl also kept defenses from clogging the line against the Patriots' strong running game by catching four touchdown passes.

Stingley's 1977 performance proved that he was far more than just a decoy for the running attack. He grabbed 39 passes for 657 yards—about one-third of New England's total pass receiving yardage

Darryl Stingley

—and five touchdowns. Remembering Darryl's all-purpose performances at Purdue, New England was not afraid to turn him loose on running plays as well. By the end of the season, his career rushing totals showed 28 carries for 244 yards—good for an 8.7 average—and two touchdowns.

The rapidly improving Stingley looked forward to an even better year in 1978. The Patriots had put together a powerful team that had the look of a Super Bowl contender. And they had sharpened their skills during the exhibition season so they would be ready for their season opener against the Washington Redskins.

One of New England's exhibition games brought them to Oakland to play the Raiders. Showing their muscle, the Patriots took a 14-7 lead in the early going and started another drive just before half-time. They moved the ball from their own 13-yard line to Oakland's 24, where they faced second down and 13 yards to go. The half was heading into its final minute when the Patriots huddled and called for a slant-in play. Many pro receivers dreaded that play, which sent them angling toward the center of the field.

For Darryl, however, it was only an unpleasant part of his job. He cut toward the middle of the field and looked for the pass. Meanwhile his college rival, Jack Tatum, had seen the play developing from his safety position. The Raider safety, a powerful 5-foot, 11-inch, 205 pounder, known as one of the hardest hitters in football, sped towards Darryl to break up the play. The ball was thrown in Stingley's direction, but it soared far out of his reach. Darryl stretched out in an all-out effort to reach the ball. At the last second, he saw Tatum coming and instinctively ducked his head.

That was a terribly unfortunate thing to do

because when Stingley collided with Tatum, his neck was caught at a bad angle. He could not get up and had to be carried off of the field and rushed to a hospital. His injury was far more serious than his teammates thought. Darryl had trouble breathing and a fever, but he still fought hard to stay alive.

Oakland coach John Madden kept watch over Darryl's progress and supported the Stingley family in the difficult days that followed. Darryl finally pulled out of danger, but the injury left him weak and weighing only 115 pounds. It was two months before the Patriot star was flown home to begin a slow process of rehabilitation. His football career was over. But even more tragically, he had been left paralyzed below the chest.

The tragedy caused many to question the rules regarding safety in pro football, for it had been a legal play that had caused Darryl's injury. The Patriots tried to replace Darryl by trading for Harold Jackson, but there was no way to erase what had happened. The stunned Patriots did not develop into the Super Bowl team that had been expected. One forward pass—that would have fallen incomplete even without the collision—in a game that did not even count had made their lives and Darryl Stingley's a little darker.

"...to eat tomorrow—
not today!"